Bourbon and Branch Water

Bourbon and Branch Water

Poems by

Cedar Koons

© 2023 Cedar Koons. All rights reserved.
This material may not be reproduced in any form, published,
reprinted, recorded, performed, broadcast,
rewritten or redistributed without
the explicit permission of Cedar Koons.
All such actions are strictly prohibited by law.

Cover design by Shay Culligan
Cover image by Edward Scheps
Author photo by Edward Scheps

ISBN: 978-1-63980-267-8
Library of Congress Control Number: 2023932330

Kelsay Books
502 South 1040 East, A-119
American Fork, Utah 84003
Kelsaybooks.com

For my sister, Katharine Carlton Ridge, 1946–2015

Acknowledgments

Special thanks to poet Sawnie Morris for her support and encouragement.

Grateful acknowledgment is made to the following publications in which poems from *Bourbon and Branch Water* appeared, sometimes in different versions:

Carrboro's 100th Birthday Poetry Anthology: "Cleaning My Daughter's Room," "Watching the Eclipse"
The New Mexico Anthology, in press: "Asylum Seekers"
The Sun Magazine: "Bound for Better" (formerly "Leaving Home"), "Squirrels" (formerly "High Priestess")
They Wrote Us a Poem: "Cleaning My Daughter's Room," "Watching the Eclipse"

Sources for the collage poem, "The End of the Drive in Utopia":

The Babur Nama by Babur
The Garlic Papers by Stanley Crawford
Village Planning in the Primitive World by Douglas Fraser
The Cidermaster of the Rio Oscuro by Harvey Frauenglass
Goat Song by Brad Kessler
Distant Neighbors: The Selected Letters of Wendell Berry and Gary Snyder by Gary Snyder and Wendell Berry

Contents

I Cherry Pop

Mayapple Time	15
Falls City 1937	16
Spencer County 1930	18
Original Sin	19
Snow Globe	21
Transfiguration	23
Labor Day at the Boat Club	26
Cherry Pop	27
The Ursuline Festival	29
Ballad for Marty	31
Bound for Better	33
Let Me In	35

II The End of the Drive in Utopia

We passed through morning	39
Hippie Wedding	40
The Day Before You Were Born	42
How Things Dry Out	44
No Word of Farewell	45
Squirrels	46
Mud Time	47
Watching the Eclipse	48
Asylum Seekers	50
Climate Refugees	52
Hungry Ghost	53
For Sudan and All His Relations	55
Cleaning My Daughter's Room	56
Ready to Leap	58
Staying Here	59

The End of the Drive in Utopia	60
Our Favorite Story	62
The Cheatham Gene	63
The Grandmother	65
Boon Companion	67
The Peace of the Barn	68

I
Cherry Pop

Mayapple Time

On the floor of the forest
the mayapples are bobbing.
Small lobed umbrellas under which
a pixie hides.
They bow in the cold winds
that flow along the ground
and tremble in the warm updrafts.
Purply green at first
the males crowd the choice wet spots
hiding in their midst
the double female, stem rising
to spread like two fans
between which a bud is poised.
As the days lengthen, the bud will swell
and open. The blossom will be waxy,
a white, five-petaled setting for
lime stamens and a golden pistil.
From this flower a fruit forms,
edible when soft though the plant is poison.
Within a yellowish skin its custard ripens slowly,
hidden by drying leaves now drooping,
coveted by chipmunks and voles.
Come August, find and eat the tart
creamy apple, accept the invitation
to dance within its brief spell
and return to playing naked and free
in the forgotten woods of childhood.

Falls City 1937

*The high water mark
from that flood
is painted above the mantle
in old buildings up and down
the Ohio River.*

Jack and Frank shared a canoe,
one they took down
the Kentucky and the Ohio,
camping and fishing,
and they kept it
in the shed behind Jack's house.
The day the river crested
Frank dropped by Jack's store,
got him to close up early
and they hauled the boat
to the top of Broadway.
They put into a river
full of logs and trash,
dead dogs and such—
Jack was cautious,
maybe they should
check with the police?
Frank was reckless, giddy,
and he prevailed.

They followed the flood
down to the Brown Hotel,
Frank looking for ladies
requiring rescue,
then down Fourth Street
where the current seethed
around sewers,
roared around corners,
tossed them against storefronts.

Cattle and pigs let loose
from the Bourbon Stockyards
were lowing, screaming,
nearly swamping the boat,
before Jack and Frank
reached high ground
at the Courthouse.
It was sunny and cold.
They sat on the grass,
ate ham sandwiches,
and enjoyed the chaos.

Jack used to call
that day an adventure,
though they lent the canoe
and never got it back.
He and Frank
drifted apart after that.
Jack was drafted in 1941.
Pearl Harbor, then
North Africa and Italy,
he rose in the ranks,
came home, raised a family,
lived to be 100.
Frank enlisted, became
a paratrooper, *of course
he would be a paratrooper,*
Jack, my father, said.
Frank dropped on D Day,
went MIA in France, 1944.
His only child
was my first love.

Spencer County 1930

Uncle John was shot in the street on market day
in cold blood, by the deputy sheriff, over a bootleg deal.
Grandpa ran from the courthouse to where he lay
in a halo of blood, pretty John, drunk and dying.

In cold blood, by the deputy sheriff, over a bootleg deal—
that deputy ran protection on every still back then.
In a halo of blood, pretty John, now dead,
Judge Cheatham's son and my mother's brother, twenty-one.

That deputy ran protection on every still back then.
The sheriff knew all of it. Poor Johnny never drew his gun.
Grandpa's firstborn, my mother's brother, twenty-one,
should've known better than to cross the likes of them.

The sheriff knew all of it. Poor Johnny never drew his gun.
He'd been drinking moonshine since he was fourteen.
Should've known better than to cross the likes of them.
John was a fool and filthy-minded, Momma said.

He'd been drinking moonshine since he was fourteen,
used to bring his floozies home for you know what.
John was a fool and filthy-minded, Momma said.
A child, she lay in her bed and listened to them.

Used to bring his floozies home for you know what.
To Judge and Grandma he could do no wrong.
A child, Momma lay in her bed and listened to them.
She didn't even know what all they did.

To Judge and Grandma he could do no wrong.
They didn't even know what all he did.
Uncle John was shot in the street on market day.
Grandpa ran from the courthouse to where he lay.

Original Sin

Bundled in my blue snowsuit
I stand on the front seat,
holding to the steering wheel,
watch my mother step
red high heels and seamed stockings
over pee-stained snow.

She flicks shiny brown hair
off her fox collar, smiles at me,
and disappears into the Sun
Chinese Laundry, to pick up
Daddy's shirts. The car is running,
heater warm, the radio
plays "The Tennessee Walz,"
I start to dance.

I bounce on the seat and gaze
at the store sign, a golden disk
sun whose face and rays
remind me of God,
the Holy Ghost whose
all-seeing eyes
stare into darkness,
see what I can't see.

Stopping still at the wheel,
I realize. I am.
The Sun illuminates me
whispers my true name,
says my life can never be
deserved or repaid.
Bounce, bounce, bounce.

Ooh, I've squished her cigarettes!
Here she comes now, she'll be mad!
She won't take me
to Woolworths' for a cherry phosphate
or home to cuddle
and listen to "Our Miss Brooks."

Ashamed, I hide
her crumpled Kents under the seat.

Snow Globe

Late in the kindergarten day
the teacher, old Mrs. Rickert,
remarks that because of the storm
we'll be sent home soon.

Dread comes over me—
Will someone come for me?
Snow clouds darken the light
of the high narrow windows.

"Who is coming for you?"
Mrs. Rickert leans down to ask,
her upper lip pulled back,
fingers digging into my arm.

Around me children are
laughing, zipping into coats,
running out to waiting cars,
bound for homes not like mine.

My hand in my jumper pocket
strokes the silky mouse they gave me
the day they took my blanket. I wet
my pants just a little. I will not cry.

"You can't wait here," Rickert whispers,
her breath like a dead bouquet. "I'll take you
to the Rectory." *The Rectory—*
the big house where the priests are.

But when she opens the door
there stands Momma, her breath ringing her
like a galactic halo, our rat terrier, Miggs,
barking, the snow blowing in a swirl.

She puts down our sled, shakes out
a red wool blanket and takes my hand.
"Climb aboard," she says, dismissing Rickert.
We fly home on shining streets.

Transfiguration

A dirty grey blanket of winter
gathers dusk as I walk home from school
to an empty house. A gloom settles.

I make a peanut butter sandwich,
sit on the floor with my homework books,
watch old war movies in black and white.

Hail batters the windows, ice slicks trees,
belying the vernal equinox I learned
about in school. I believed it meant

spring should have come already, today
to end whatever this is that makes
it hard to think, a suffocation

sitting on my chest like a bully,
tv gun fire in the background.
Alone, I turn on lights in every room.

My sisters come home, go upstairs and
talk behind closed doors, boyfriends,
the curse, their new piano duet.

Parents are home. Dinner is ready.
Fish croquettes, peas and a glass of milk
in the cramped, stuffy kitchen, silent

except for chewing and swallowing.
Momma grades tests and papers,
Daddy drinks brandy and reads novels.

My arithmetic is left undone.
Each day the same in endless winter.
Up before dawn, my grey uniform

the grey stone school, the grey concrete
steps where the popular girls gather.
The playground, cruel boys, choosing teams.

I slip into the church, its nave dark, still,
fragrant with frankincense and beeswax.
I walk the stations of the cross, pray

at each bas relief in olive wood.
Jesus, his passion, his beloveds,
his path of suffering beckoning me.

Veronica waits to wipe dark blood
from a face contorted by a crown's
cruel thorns. Mary, Stabat Mater,

dying Dismas, the good thief, begging,
John's adoration and despair as
Jesus gives up his spirit. The sky

and earth split open, the dead emerge.
I hear the recess bells calling me,
back to a long, sleepy afternoon.

The class has memorized a poem,
"I wandered lonely as a cloud," one
by one, we recite it. It drones on

forever. Just before dismissal
light pricks through the grey, and blue sky appears.
Clouds tremble, transfigure and dissolve

swept aside by frenzied, freshened winds.
I put on my coat and run outside.
The grass is shamrock green, the mud shines,

the air smells like crisp, clean sheets and I
can hear the wind in wings of pigeons.
A man is selling flowers, buckets of

yellow daffodils, thousands of jonquils
swaying in the breeze like the spirit
of God over the waters, scent of

stamen and pistil to prove it's spring,
rhyming resurrection with buried bulbs
that rise up golden. I gaze and gaze.

Labor Day at the Boat Club

The pop-pop of tennis balls from the busy courts.
Boaters coming up and going down to the docks.
Tables are set up by the Negro staff,
white tablecloths, silver plate set out
for the last supper of summer.
Standing rib roast, fried chicken, green beans,
coleslaw, chess pie, sweet tea.
John, the head waiter, greeting the members.

Even the barflies out on the terrace
carry their old-fashioneds to the tables
to drink in the gathering dusk.
I'm shivering in my wet swimsuit.
Tomorrow is back to school,
itchy uniforms, bad-tempered nuns.
Tomorrow is Pinesol-scented confinement,
early Mass, work sheets, piano lessons,
the priest at catechism standing too close.

Catching minnows and gar in cups,
canoeing to Six Mile Island,
swim meets and spend-the-nights,
goodbye, goodbye to all that.
Next year I'll have breasts,
I'll drop off the swim team, play cards,
smoke cigarettes, and get boy-crazy.

Tonight, I stand in the dusk and watch the lights
on the water, restless like the water
in that blue, blue pool.

Cherry Pop

Picture a small Southern town in the fifties,
the shady streets near a college campus,
my house next door to Grandma's
on a dead end, with woods and creeks, remnants
of country estates and farms, close
to an uptown of shops, an A & P,
Woolworth's with a lunch counter, a dress shop
and a movie theatre called The Vogue.
At the center of my world
is me, a tomboy, small, and plain, without
fear. I walk to school, to church, I see
when someone takes note of me
and mostly they don't. This town,
so Penny Lane, so Mayberry,
even the local pervert who exposes
himself seems rosy.

I know who owns each house and the names
of the dogs running loose and
the ironing ladies and maids
waiting at the bus stop to go to their
part of town, looking tired and old.
I am a white girl whose parents work and
drink. Allowed out until dark, I roam alone
abandoned fields and barns, framed-in houses
in new neighborhoods and slip, a shadow,
in and out of stores, drinking cherry cokes
at the soda fountain, stealing gum,
comic books, a Tootsie Roll, a pack
of Parliaments left on a counter. Now
I'm twelve. I endure the catcalls of the hoods
on the corner. I'm goosed in Woolworth's,
teased by boys in line at The Vogue.

At the Boat Club, fathers of girls I know
stare at my new breasts displayed in
a wet swimsuit, their sons take me for rides
with Early Times and water. Older boys
have a taste for little virgins like me. I don't favor
the boys my age, boys from St. X, nice boys
with sweaty hands and slobbery kisses.
I prefer older boys, men even, suave,
dangerous, who know what makes a cherry
pop. *There was a girl in your ninth-grade class
picked up after school by such a man
and never seen again*. But I am lucky—

I always have mad money just in case
a guy gets weird. I love the risk
but I'm not stupid, or so I think.
Only later do I wonder at close
calls that felt exciting, like the time
that man I met at the Boat Club docks
took me on his Cabin Cruiser
and kept me out all night.
My parents make new rules
which I ignore. I'll not
be like my sister, married
at nineteen, pregnant
and miserable.
I am careful and wise
to the game. I'll study hard.
And when I get away from here—
I'll get away for good.

The Ursuline Festival

Tonight the nuns have a party.
Bring your money, anything goes.

A Ferris wheel lights up the sky. A
tattooed man makes it surge.

Tall Sr. Mercia works the St. Agnes booth, a
wad of bills in her big hand.

Tatted pillowcases made by the ancient ones
leave in the pockets of bachelors and altar boys.

At the Archdiocese booth, Brother Bill smokes a
cigar, rolls the dice, yells, "Put your money down,

win a rosary or a portrait of the Pope." On
the flying swings, pretty Sr. Portia, (the one

with the slight mustache) sits beside Father
Flynn, the one you want for confession.

Sister Bernard, who sleeps through Latin class,
looks on, wide awake. The roller coaster,

a blur of lights, roars behind the Chapel.
Couples neck on benches by the narthex door.

The Sanctuary, lit by perpetual light, smells
like frankincense and bubblegum. No one is at prayer.

Behind the Motherhouse the athletic field is dewy.
St. X boys and Sacred Heart girls walk barefoot

hand in hand. Someone will pick a cherry under
the bleachers. Someone will leave her

underpants in the wet grass.
The moon looks on like a voyeur.

Ballad for Marty

She wasn't in the smart class,
we were never really friends,
people called her ways "fast,"
I loved her wild poems.

She brought her work to *Tapers,*
our high school magazine,
I printed some I favored,
she was happy, or it seemed.

That spring she acted wicked
and seldom showed at school,
had run-ins with the Sisters,
I thought she was a fool.

Her mother was a waitress
and her father was a drunk,
she'd likely sealed her fate
with some plebeian punk.

Back then you got knocked up
if you couldn't figure how
to get the guy to stop,
so what could she do now?

I'd been there once myself,
ten weeks or near about,
but Daddy found a way,
to take the problem out.

Because I had rich parents
I was bound for better things,
to college and beyond,
with luck as well as brains.

But she was staring down a fate,
a home for unwed mothers:
"Hide away and cry your shame,
then give your child to others."

She couldn't make him marry,
she couldn't go to school,
fate would snuff her dreams out,
that was the white trash rule.

It was just before commencement
when the dogwoods were in bloom,
that her shape gave her away,
and we knew that she was doomed.

She ran into the car lot
with her friends all running after,
the whole school heard the gunshot
that caused her head to shatter.

Put down your white diplomas,
girls, put down your red, red roses,
remember for a moment
how this wild girl got broken.

Bound for Better

In the living room the tv was on.
I sat on a sofa against a green afghan
until she was ready for me.
Her husband drank a beer,
told me not to touch the shivering chihuahua.
"She's got a mean bite," he said.

Aunt Wanda's husband
found this woman. His truck drivers
recommended her. My father, a good Catholic,
drove me there, just like he took me
to confession other Friday evenings.
In her bedroom, pictures of grandchildren
cluttered the dresser, white stockings
hung on a wooden rack above
white shoes newly polished.
She had me lie on the double bed.

Opening my legs for her wasn't easy.
She was hunched and burnt-looking.
Her whole face puckered toward her mouth.
She mumbled something like "dirty shame,"
while she gave her absolution,
a small white cloth inserted into my cervix.
I wanted it to hurt. It didn't at first,
not even the needle she pushed
into my thigh, while I watched my hand
curl and uncurl the chenille bedspread.

The first blood came before dawn.
My father went to work.
My mother watched tv.
I lay upstairs and thought of college
as rhythmic pains came.

I turned my crucifix to the wall
and soaked the sheets.
Just after lunch I passed the cloth,
some clots, some flesh.
I bundled it in a clean towel
and lay on the yellow bathroom rug.
I will go away from here, I sang to myself,
I will never come back. I will never come back.

Let Me In

You said we'd go before
I left for fall semester.
Don't go back to sleep!
I have your mug of coffee,
I've got your cigarettes,
I've already fed the horses,
got the tack! Wake
up, get dressed.
I've packed a lunch, filled
our canteens, got chocolates
and peppermint schnapps.
Don't be a pain,
get up, unlock your door!
I'll saddle Dot, help
you with Lolly, come on!
Let's laugh about last night,
we were both drunk, right? I know
we argued, okay, it's my fault.
It's our last morning.
My car is packed—

Let's go while it's still cool,
let's trespass over to McRae's,
there's mist on his hayfield
but the ground is good and dry.
Remember last spring
how Lolly bucked and Dot
took off down a wet trail?
Lucky Dot didn't pull a tendon.
So fun! Hey, maybe there are morels
where we found them last fall. Remember?
Won't you come?
I won't be back till Christmas,
if then! Carlton, why
won't you let me in?

II

The End of the Drive in Utopia

We passed through morning

as if every day were perfect
for picking strawberries.
Forenoons like moist hayfields
full of tender heads of grain
and nests of meadowlarks.
Sex was tart, plump, sweet, casual.
We tasted of beautiful fruit, firm and ripe.

By afternoon our bodies
floated before us, omnipotent,
and at dusk we lay down,
sleepy, lustrous, and slick.
Under a moon always waxing
we held to our secret dreams—
clear as water in a rocked spring,
certain as promises we made,
and as carelessly forgotten.

Hippie Wedding

They found each other young and could not wait,
they walked out Piney Mountain to be wed.
Four parents trailed behind accepting fate,
their dog, the maid of honor, ran ahead.

They walked out Piney Mountain to be wed,
and stood above the mist on New Hope Creek.
Their dog, the maid of honor, ran ahead.
They'd been engaged for just about a week.

They stood above the mist on New Hope Creek.
Doves in treetops cooed *this love will last.*
They'd been engaged for just about a week.
A barred owl hooted from below, *'twill pass.*

Doves in treetops cooed *this love will last,*
but they were young and focused in the now.
A barred owl hooted from below, *'twill pass.*
They spoke their truth in vague, handwritten vows.

They were young and focused in the now,
and time would lead away from youthful fun.
They spoke their truth in vague, handwritten vows,
while someone played and sang "Here Comes the Sun."

And time would lead away from youthful fun,
they'd build a cabin far from anywhere.
While someone played and sang, "Here Comes the Sun,"
a pastor made a hopeful Jesus prayer.

They'd build a cabin far from anywhere,
raise two kids and break each other's hearts.
A pastor made a hopeful Jesus prayer,
but after twenty years they'd have to part.

Raised two kids and broke each other's hearts,
they loved as best they could through many tears.
Though after twenty years they had to part,
they'd celebrate this day for fifty years.

They loved as best they could through many tears.
Their children trailed behind accepting fate.
They celebrate this day for fifty years.
They found each other young and could not wait.

The Day Before You Were Born

Indian summer, hot and sticky.
Poplars gold, sassafras crimson
cumulonimbus white as communion,
foretelling a change in the weather.

The last cutting of hay lies baled.
Grey green timothy cubes
tossed down a long narrow field
to feed three heifers due to freshen.

The crickets sing and mist rises
above a river where chill gathers
and an owl voices concern. I drive
the truck, squeezed into the cab,

my overdue belly pressed
against the steering wheel.
Our friends lift bale after bale
until twilight when the moon pokes out.

The last day of time. The
last day of me before you
breathed in all I'd always known.
You turn in my body, unable to settle.

We drink cider going to hard
and cold buttermilk, eat salty cornbread.
I ask Joy if she is also pregnant and
she says yes, only just knowing it.

When the bales are put up,
we slip into the Eno, deep and still.
Itch and sweat wash into chills.
I watch your knees ripple

under my skin. Time
slides into place like a gear
driving the old story, showing
the blood that makes it new.

How Things Dry Out

High pressure for days, the sky
enameled. Mayapples go to seed
and fade to yellow shriveled stalks.
Tulip poplars, deserted by bees,
drop woody flowers, and spring
though not yet over, no longer sings.

The baby in my belly feels heavy
as a basket of wet laundry. You're
gone at dawn, back at dusk, not much
to say. At midday the garden
droops. The squash bugs have arrived.
My toddler and I play Old Maid

then nap together on the couch.
I pitch hay to the horses, gather
the hen eggs, punch down the bread dough.
Flies buzz in the milk bottles.
I wonder how our moist spring
set us up for this dryness.

Dreaming of the mountains,
cliffs catching clouds, bluets in July,
rain on my skin, afternoon delight,
a swim in a cold river—I need
to hear thunder rolling and
feel the earth get soaked.

No Word of Farewell

In the sticky heat of late afternoon,
our toddler sleeps in the hammock. Cicadas
whine in the trees. In the fall garden,
you plant turnips and collards.

From deep woods the dove calls,
a sound to me that's sad.
"Summer is over," the bird seems to say.
"A loss is coming." Today

we robbed the bees, removed the best
of their spring labor but left a little lest
they go hungry next winter. Honeycomb
in mason jars, a heavy crown to laden shelves.

On the front porch our daughter sings
"Wildwood Flower," strums a ukulele.
Our eldest spots deer along the creek, where he's
apt to go at chore time. He says he's seen

the six-point buck he'll hunt
come November. It's cooler now, nearly dark.
Squirrels on the roof skitter
in demented circles. Everyone is hungry.

Days go by without a touch.
My body toughens to weather
winter. Time to shut the henhouse.
Below a scratch of moon, Venus burns.

Squirrels

Our first appointment,
with our third therapist
late on a Friday afternoon.

She offers a couch but
you choose the black chair
near the door. I settle
in a dark corner where
a Ficus is dying.
"What brings you here?"
We peel off our
bandages for her to see.

Who knew she'd be so capable?
Honed like a good knife,
in one session
she cuts us cleanly
out of our marriage.

Once I watched
a country neighbor expertly
skin a squirrel.
"Done one, you done 'em all."
A slice and a tug and
the pelt tears loose.
Almost no blood.

Mud Time

after Evening at Kuerner's by Andrew Wyeth

The year my husband left life fell apart.
March sleet turned into epic sucking mud.
The Datsun stuck sideways and wouldn't start—
which meant I wouldn't get to work. A flood
of needs I couldn't meet flowed in. Alone
most nights I listened to the rain.
While children slept I settled into stone,
but numbness only amplified the pain.
That tactic never really worked so well.
One night I took a spade and dug the muck
that trapped my car and life into a hell.
I dug and spun, reversed and drove, unstuck
at last. I saw my strength, how hard, how true,
how to begin to make myself anew.

Watching the Eclipse

The first full moon after
the vernal equinox I sit
on my front porch
drinking whiskey and
watching the eclipse.
The cat has killed
something and cracks
its bones under the stoop.
At my feet the dog runs
in her sleep. Inside, my
phone machine gives voice
in the empty room.
I think about what you said
about how good love
can turn around and bite you
harder than none at all.
This is what I think
as the shadow of Earth
covers the moon.
I recognize the voice
on the machine. It is
my ex-husband. He is
going on and on, as he does,
and then I realize it is really
my son, who sounds so
much like him. But when
I get to the phone
he has hung up. I can't call
him back. He wanted a ride
somewhere. Anyway, I am
too drunk to drive.

Now the moon looks new.
I think about my work,
how I love it but don't want
to do it, and about the faces
and voices of my patients
how they enter my office
and all they want is
someone to listen,
someone who won't judge.
I go through boxes
of government tissue.

Slowly, the shadow lifts itself
off the moon. Stars go dim
again, a second twilight. Sirens,
traffic noise, intensify. I think
of you in Myrtle Beach
some topless bar, some motel.
I think of what you said
about love and I disagree.
Nothing takes a bite out of you
worse than no love at all.

Asylum Seekers

I sit with you, little immigrant child, near
where deputies in bullet-proof vests stare
at monitors and lawyers huddle in tense clots
with coffee, outside the courtroom. I hold
your dimpled hand, grubby Elmo between us.
You absently suck your thumb and stroke
the side of my breast, a stream of snot
slick under your nose, both of us
engulfed in the buzz of fluorescent lights,
the clanging of doors, the sound of chains
on the ankles of men shuffled in one door
and out the other, the chatter and laughter
of functionaries.   You are my third today—
I cannot pronounce your name, a name
no one calls you anymore, in a language
no one here speaks. You have a number on your
file instead. For our short interaction I want
to be a cloth mother to you, little monkey,
but warned as I am against touching you
when your tiny body and brown eyes cry out
touch me, I am really the wire mother.
I read in your file you came from Honduras
with your flesh mother, a criminal, they say,
from whom you were taken. Because of all this
you no longer speak and wear diapers
which now need changing.

Finding you without your mother
is like finding a human heart on the street,
still beating, or an exotic hummingbird
blown down to a rocky beach
in a hurricane, lost in migration,

lost to all context, to the continuity
we call being alive, lost to faces
and smells, corn, milk, things making sense.
And there are so many of you!
Little hand, we are both afraid, don't tell.
I cling to you and imagine I am somehow
protecting you and saving myself. But
I can read the signs. I know better.

Climate Refugees

Glaciers groan, break apart, weakened by deep ice melting.
We burn through their teal calves, floes and bergs, ice melting.

We turn away as our cousins, the white bears, gray whales,
and coral reefs disappear, hope and solace melting.

Our forests explode in blazing whirls, white hot twisters,
fire winds that rocket to the upper air, heights melting.

Songbirds flee the ocean flyway, blown down by thousands,
delicate yellow-green warblers found in ice, melting.

Tonight, crack open a single malt, smoky amber,
numb this aching, make the brain make nice, melting.

Drink to a bony moon held glimmering, resolve to live
true to all goddesses named, unnamed, while night is melting.

Warm winds promise an early thaw, whooshing.
In the cedar grove where magpies roost, make rites for melting.

Hungry Ghost

Carlton said her mind was like a serpent eating
its tail. That afternoon she drove on country
roads near home and found a pawnshop.
Their camera showed she came and went, unsure,
but finally bought a "lady's gun,"
looked for a spot off the road to die.

A bad game of craps, roll of a broken die.
At midnight I was in the kitchen eating,
unable to sleep. I didn't think she'd buy a gun.
My other sister called, they'd searched the country,
called the state police, tried her phone, unsure
they'd find her alive. I thought about the pawnshop

near her farm. She stopped by that pawnshop,
then drove and drove searching as the die
rolled. She found a farm road, drove down it, unsure,
lit a cigarette and smoked. She hadn't eaten
yet that day. Around her the bluegrass country
she loved. She locked her car, took the gun.

To take life quickly, efficiently, a gun
is needed. Buy one easily in any pawnshop.
Ready, she sat under a tree in the country
of the lost, the muzzle to her brow to die.
At dawn I called the state trooper, he was eating.
Did he say search party? I was unsure.

She was gone before the mist rose. We were unsure
she wasn't still alive. But she was slumped against that tree, gun
in her hand. She'd written the note "the serpent eating
its tail" on a receipt from the pawnshop.

Did she regret her choice as she lay dying?
Has she became a hungry ghost in bardo country?

Once she loved her life, her home, a country
of rolling pastures, winsome as she was. But unsure
how to silence the crazy voices, she had to die
to escape the serpent tongue, was reminded of a gun
by noticing an open roadside pawnshop,
poisoned by despair that she'd been eating.

She'd already decided to die, eating her fear.
I see her in a country pawnshop
buying the gun, still unsure.

For Sudan and All His Relations

O Sudan, your armored body, huge white head
and improbable horns (good for rheumatism, as a status
symbol or to make a ceremonial dagger), have led
desperate men to kill your kind. You leave us

only your image in extinction's bestiary, with long
lashes to placid black eyes, an unmistakable outline
torn from the nursery's savanna, one so strong
you could walk unharmed among hungry lions.

You shared grasslands with elephants and cheetahs
soon to follow you in the great extinction called Anthropocene.
Take your place among the dodo, mammoth and moa.
Don't worry though, we'll somehow save your genes!

Chief Seattle warned us we would die like this, lonely,
once we'd murdered all our animal friends. It is now too late
for you, White Rhino, and maybe for Sapiens, last of genus homo,
who cannot evolve in time to survive such self-destructive traits.

Cleaning My Daughter's Room

When I open the door, one shade is
down, and one up like a wink
goodbye. The bed is unmade
and last semester's books lie
in a pile at the foot, and strewn around
are assorted socks and undies.
You're gone, but it looks
like you're taking a shower, be back
in a minute. For years after I left
home, my room, too, was arranged
just the way I left it. My clothes on the floor
of the closet, the burn mark on the white
dresser from a cigarette.

After Christmas we drive
to Kentucky, over mountains, through tunnels,
and I watch you sleep, stretched out,
unaware of me or the car. On in the dark,
past seething refineries and across
wide black rivers into country empty
of people. I listen to your breathing, think
of my mother, her tiny, breathless voice over the phone,
in the room with her oxygen and TV.

In her day, my mother looked
like Katherine Hepburn and had great legs.
Our albums are full of her bathing suit shots.
Always slender, now she's skeletal.
Daddy talks about how cute she was, and frets
over what she'll eat. She loves you,
you take after her, she says, smart, stylish.
You go right in, sit beside her,

discuss her Siamese cats over the din
of the TV. I can't take it. I'll clean the upstairs
to keep from turning off the racket
and asking her if she's really ready
for this, doesn't she want to
talk about stuff, make a plan?

For you, Daughter, another semester has begun.
An intermezzo, your salad days, brief golden age.
Spring break in Boston, summer job in New York,
next year abroad. I think of something I overheard
you say to a friend, "It's always the same here.
I think it's going to be different, but it's the same."
I put down the other blind, change the sheets and dust,
rearrange your dresser as I like it, symmetrical.
I feel like an acrobat, the steady one on the bottom,
holding the ones light as air, ready to leap.

Ready to Leap

after Woody Guthrie

Luis comes to pull the weeds in my garden,
Jesus digs a trench, and we laugh at his name,
The men who wait for work at the corner,

When the music stops, one will be gone.

Pilar comes to care for my child in the morning,
Jazmín comes each week to scrub down my floors.
These women alone have families waiting,

When the music stops, one will be gone.

We don't see the cow walk into the gun,
we don't see the needle go into the dog,
we don't see the migrants climb into the vans,

we just look away and they disappear.

Like musical chairs their options will dwindle,
when one is deported another arrives,
Adíos, José! Hello, Rosalita!

Here is some money, now please disappear.

Staying Here

Raw winds, late wet snow
                risotto and shitake mushrooms
robins and waxwings feast on crabapples
                slow burning wet wood fire smokes
ristra blows sideways on the front porch.
                My love is cooking dinner, jazz on the radio
I come from the greenhouse
                with spinach, kale, daikon and thyme
Jicarita is wreathed in weather
                we watch from the banco with cabernet
as the valley is washed & sugared—
                will we go out or stay in?
Snow on the tongue & river song, or
                make love, eat, take the day's measure?
We enter the wordless stream
                of bodily pleasure, buoyed and anchored
by the privilege of being here.

The End of the Drive in Utopia

Wherever paradise exists, so does the idea that it was lost.
Our ability to stay present with the chaos may in the end be our
salvation.

Our camp circle was like the circle of stars in the heavens.
The stars: what are they? Holes in the great curtain between us and
an ocean of light *and no self whatever.*

The moment the calf is born it is plucked from its mother and she
is sent to be milked.
Elk mother and calf swim in the river right in front of our canoes.

The goat reached back toward his stiffened penis, lifted a hind leg,
and shot urine into his mouth!
Pan is the only god said to have died.

The air rests on darkness;
*We'll have plenty of apricots this year. I'll let you know when they
start to fall*
but what the darkness rests on, only God knows.

We emerged out of mystery and back into mystery we return.
*I seem to have to work harder, travel more
and be gone forever.*

Banditry and lawlessness were commonplace when *that* plague
raged. Politics, like nature, abhors a vacuum.
What kind of economy will cherish trees?

Keeping myself and the whole farm in place, breathing,
counting my breaths.
Coffee is bound to become prohibitively expensive.

My language is formed by the pantry and the gate, the rose and the lily,
the dog and the fish and the tiger, the clouds and the stones.

If I've learned anything in this long life, it is that anger can lure you into a cave of
blindness and ignorance from which it is often difficult to find a way out.

Our ability to stay present with the chaos may in the end be our salvation.
Wherever paradise exists, so does the idea that it was lost.

Our Favorite Story

In this story rivers have huge beaver lodges and flotillas
of ducks. Fish teem under every snag, and no one bothers them.

In this story the skies are pitch and the stars have actual faces.
Dogs roam in packs at night and no one bothers them.

In this story there is lots of snow. Lakes freeze solid,
bison cross them single file and no one bothers them.

In this story prairies roar with wind and herds stampede,
fires burn for years, and no one bothers them.

In this story boreal forests creep down from the tundra
bringing white tigers and snow leopards and no one bothers them.

This story has no history, no songs, no poems, no sagas.
There are many dead, but no one bothers them.

In this story there is no one to tell this story.

The Cheatham Gene

My daughter is visiting with her fiancé.
It's August and full monsoon.
The desert is grey-green and golden,
the garden full of tomatoes and snakes.

My father sent my mother's wedding dress.
preserved in a sealed blue box,
visible through a brittle plastic window,
untouched since my sister wore it in 1965.

Thunder rumbles. My daughter opens the box.
An anvil of cloud in the east. The dress
unfolds from tissue paper, a fragile antique
with a silk bodice and a lace train.

She holds the champagne-colored
Chantilly lace against her white skin.
Steps into it as wind rattles the blinds.
I button up the back like in an old movie.

The lace is stiff and yellowed.
My mother saved for this dress,
teaching "up on Briar Ridge" where
she lived with a different family each week.

My parents were married in August.
They sweltered in St. Bridget's Church.
My father in his wool dress uniform.
My mother in this heavy dress and veil,

98 pounds with a small waist,
big bosoms and dark wavy hair.
The dress fits my slender girl.
I'm built sturdy like my Daddy.

She is determined, particular.
She has the "Cheatham gene" we like to say
to describe a certain quality my mother's people had.
They were bright, funny people, hard workers

and whiskey drinkers, mercurial
ambitious, secretive and sharp,
always well-dressed.
She's buttoned perfectly into the gown.

She walks slowly, with lots of rustling, to the mirror.
Outside it is finally raining, really coming down.
She sighs, looks at her reflection.
With my father gone in the war, my mother

moved back to Spencer County
to live with her parents
until the war was over.
My daughter turns in the mirror.

I can see from her face
she won't wear this dress. She owns
herself and unlike my mother
she'll get the wedding she wants.

The dress will go back to the attic.
My sister will take it away when
we clear my father's house.
The evening is cool and the rain over.

My husband opens a bottle of champagne.
My daughter is relieved to have this done.
She knows she's free to make her choices.
That heirloom was passed down long ago.

The Grandmother

She has few worries yet.
Her ankles are strong.
She walks the uneven ground steady, without fear.
She hears and names the birds,
knows what star that is,
what snake, who of those born
most favor those who've died.

She had a second chance in her forties
after seven years alone, married again,
moved out west, helped to raise
his sons. Left behind a whole life
for someone who would love her body.
They've made their peace with age, with touch
and talk and release with laughter. She knows
one will leave, the date unknown but certain.
She thinks it might not be as hard
as when it seemed life was forever.
But it might be harder now when death feels close.

She knows the days that begin
with a long swim in icy water
will not return, though she have twenty
more Julys. She almost hopes she doesn't.
The things she based her faith upon
have vanished, but faith remains,
a habit, a shield hanging in her ancestral home,
a light left on for a return after dark.
She paddles on the empty lake, her arms
given to the work
as her eyes are to the moonrise.
She knows what comes:

goodbye to the lake and her canoe,
goodbye to a good gallop, the tenderest touch
goodbye to what she claims of strength or beauty.
She has just begun to consider conversations
she wants to have with those long dead.

Boon Companion

My daughter's child, a girl of ten, content
to play for hours at home with books and pens,
her stuffies and costumes, her Gran. Time spent
in play together has no clock, not tense
like motherhood, with cooking, picking up.
Too soon her chores and homework, beaux and peers,
will steal our afternoons, take the last lap
of her short run of childhood and leave me here
fixed in her amber past. I hear her voice,
a bell marking our time. I stroke the gold
on her smooth, white back. An impending loss
feels near. Her growing up twins my growing old.
My world begins to die as hers is born.
We glide on paths uncharted and unknown.

The Peace of the Barn

Horses doze in stalls deep in new shavings.
Flies buzz in the empty sweet feed buckets.
The barn cat stretches on the highest bale.
All the riders have gone.
The arena gate stands open.
The tack room is tidy, bridles
and saddles each in their places.
All the water troughs are full.
Old Maisie, not long for this world
stands in her stall, face to the wall.
The metal roof crackles in the heat.
Big thunderheads mass in the east.
Swallows swoop in and out under the eaves.
It will soon be suppertime.

My paint gelding stands on three legs
and gives a contented blow.
I give him a curry and brushing,
feed a whole bag of carrots one at a time,
comb his mane and tail, pick his feet.
He turns his neck to lay his nose in my hand,
gives me a soft look from his big eye.
Another day gone and no loss.
It's good to be sound though old,
safe and dry in an orderly place
with few demands and all you need.
Another day we'll go for a wild ride,
risk the risks that prey animals face
and run hard on the bones that define us.
But not today. Already Mauricio
is coming with the grain
and the big clouds are letting down
their full load of bright, fragrant rain.

About the Author

Cedar Koons was born and raised in Louisville, Kentucky. She graduated from Duke University with a B.A. in English in 1971 and taught English and creative writing at the high school and college level. From 1988–1993 she was poet in residence at Duke University Medical Center where she edited the chapbooks, *I Want to Read You a Poem* and *They Wrote Us a Poem* and led a weekly poetry group in the Duke University Medical School. She served on the board of The North Carolina Writer's Network and was a member of the Black Socks Poets.

In 1993, Cedar received her M.S.W. from the University of North Carolina at Chapel Hill. For thirty years, she worked as a psychotherapist, consultant, and trainer, specializing in the treatment of borderline personality disorder (BPD) using Dialectical Behavior Therapy (DBT) and still maintains a small practice. She published numerous academic and research articles and book chapters on the practice of DBT.

Cedar has published a nonfiction book, *The Mindfulness Solution for Intense Emotions: Take Control of BPD with DBT* (New Harbinger, 2016), and a novel, *Murder at Sleeping Tiger,* (as C. R. Koons, Camel Press, 2022). *Bourbon and Branch Water* is her first book of poetry.

Cedar is married to Edward Scheps, a photographer, and they have four children and four grandchildren. They live in Dixon, New Mexico, on a small farm on the Rio Embudo. You can follow Cedar's occasional blog at www.cedarkoons.com.

www.ingramcontent.com/pod-product-compliance
Lightning Source LLC
Chambersburg PA
CBHW030914170426
43193CB00009BA/839